MW00980283

A BASIC BOOK OF
COCKATIELS
LOOK-AND-LEARN

by
LINDA A. LINDNER

The following is a list of photographers whose work appears in this book: Michael Gilroy, N. Richmond, R. Pearcy, Horst Bielfeld, Glen Axelrod, Cliff Beckford, Louise Van der Meld, Vince Serbin, William Parlee, A. Kerstitch, Dr. H.R. Axelrod, John Marigione, J. Donahue, N. Reed, B. Kahle, Jack Harris, Ray Hansen, Fred Harris, Mark Runnals, Wayne Wallace, Michael DeFreitas, E. Goldfinger, J. Manzione, J. Sturman, Dr. Allen, Vogelpark Walsrode, Jerry Kessler, Rebecca Brega, W. Loeding, Louise Bauck. Illustrations by artist John Quinn.
Cover photograph of a Cinnamon Pearl Cockatiel by Michael Gilroy

Distributed in the UNITED STATES to the Pet Trade by T.F.H. Publications, Inc., One T.F.H. Plaza, Neptune City, NJ 07753; distributed in the UNITED STATES to the Bookstore and Library Trade by National Book Network, Inc. 4720 Boston Way, Lanham MD 20706; in CANADA to the Pet Trade by H & L Pet Supplies Inc., 27 Kingston Crescent, Kitchener, Ontario N2B 2T6; Rolf C. Hagen Ltd., 3225 Sartelon Street, Montreal 382 Quebec; in CANADA to the Book Trade by Macmillan of Canada (A Division of Canada Publishing Corporation), 164 Commander Boulevard, Agincourt, Ontario M1S 3C7; in the United Kingdom by T.F.H. Publications, PO Box 15, Waterlooville PO7 6BQ; in AUSTRALIA AND THE SOUTH PACIFIC by T.F.H. (Australia), Pty. Ltd., Box 149, Brookvale 2100 N.S.W., Australia; in NEW ZEALAND by Brooklands Aquarium Ltd. 5 McGiven Drive, New Plymouth, RD1 New Zealand; in Japan by T.F.H. Publications, Japan—Jiro Tsuda, 10-12-3 Ohjidai, Sakura, Chiba 285, Japan; in SOUTH AFRICA by Multipet Pty. Ltd., P.O. Box 35347, Northway, 4065, South Africa. Published by T.F.H. Publications, Inc.
Manufactured in the United States of America by T.F.H. Publications, Inc.

SUGGESTED READING

  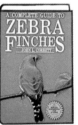 

T.F.H. offers the most comprehensive selections of books dealing with pet birds. A selection of significant titles is presented here; they and the thousands of other animal books published by T.F.H. are available at the same place you bought this one, or write to us for a free catalog.

T.F.H. Publications
One T.F.H. Plaza
Third & Union Avenues
Neptune, NJ 07753

SUGGESTED READING

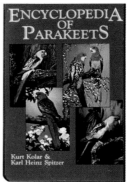

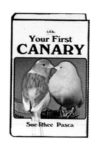

INTRODUCTION

The cockatiel is a medium-sized Australian parrot, averaging approximately 12-14 inches from the top of its head to the tip of its tail. It has come to exist in various distinctive color varieties, which give it quite a different appearance from the wild gray it originated from. Most commonly, cockatiels are of gray or white coloring with a pretty patch of marigold-orange on the cheek. Their head is capped by a crest.

A cockatiel that is allowed out of its cage will naturally take flight and explore its surroundings. A careful eye must be kept while the bird is out to ensure that it does not cause destruction to valuables. ◀

Cockatiels enjoy the companionship of other birds and of humans. If you are not able to be home all day, provide plenty of toys for your bird's entertainment.
◀

INTRODUCTION

Most people enjoy the companionship of cockatiels. They have very agreeable personalities and are intelligent as well as affectionate. The cockatiel makes an ideal pet for those who wish a bird larger than a budgie yet smaller than an amazon. A cockatiel can truly become one's best friend!

▶ Cockatiels kept in captivity must be given a nutritious, well-balanced diet that provides nutrients found in the diet of all wild birds. This includes seeds, greenfood, and tablefood.

Cockatiels are inquisitive creatures who tend to investigate everything before they approach it. A new accessory added to the cage may be left untouched for a few days until the bird becomes accustomed to it. ▶

The cockatiel does not have the brilliancy of coloration as most other parrots; it has a subdued beauty all its own. ◀

HISTORY

Pied Cockatiels often vary greatly in their plumage patterns. A symmetrical pattern is often most desirable. No two Pied Cockatiels have the same markings. ◀

The Normal Gray Cockatiel hen is colored more dully than the male. All young birds look similar to adult females; it is not until the first molt that the male attains his coloration. ◀

◀ Birds frequently bred in captivity over a long period of time usually produce a number of different color varieties. This bird is a Pearl Cockatiel.

The cockatiel was first discovered in eastern Australia in 1770. It did not become popular until the discovery of gold in the early 19th century, which brought many immigrants to the land.

By 1864, the cockatiel was well known as a household pet and within 20 years it was established as an extremely good breeding bird in European aviaries. Soon after, the cockatiel became despised because of its notoriety as a "beginner's bird." It simply tamed too easily! It was not until the introduction of mutations that the cockatiel began to experience a "rebirth" in its popularity. The interest in the new color varieties raised the demand on breeders. Today, cockatiels are available in many different varieties and the choice of a bird is truly a matter of preference.

A beautiful Normal, gray-colored male cockatiel. Although not as exotically colored as the mutations, the Normal is still the most readily available and frequently kept cockatiel. ▲

The Lutino Cockatiel is a domestically bred bird and one of the oldest cockatiel mutations. The first Lutino mutation occurred in the United States. ▶

COCKATIELS AS PETS

Cockatiels are as individual in their personalities as any humans might be. For the most part, they are extremely intelligent and affectionate animals.

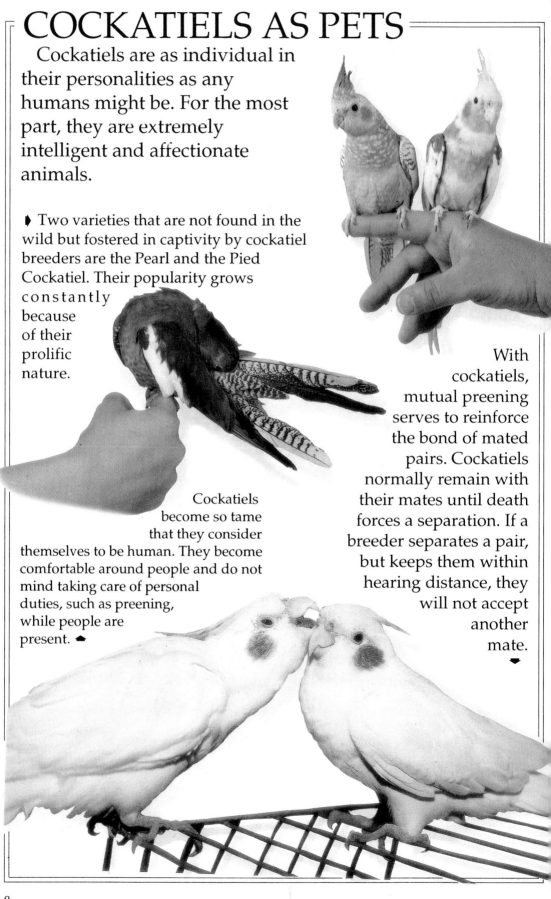

◗ Two varieties that are not found in the wild but fostered in captivity by cockatiel breeders are the Pearl and the Pied Cockatiel. Their popularity grows constantly because of their prolific nature.

Cockatiels become so tame that they consider themselves to be human. They become comfortable around people and do not mind taking care of personal duties, such as preening, while people are present. ◆

With cockatiels, mutual preening serves to reinforce the bond of mated pairs. Cockatiels normally remain with their mates until death forces a separation. If a breeder separates a pair, but keeps them within hearing distance, they will not accept another mate. ◆

COCKATIELS AS PETS

Once a cockatiel learns to trust and know you, you have a pet and companion that will last a lifetime! Each bird's individual personality develops through interaction with its owner. The majority of cockatiels love to have their heads, necks, and chins scratched. They are incredibly adaptable pets. For the apartment or condominium dweller the cockatiel makes a perfect pet because its cry is not loud or shrilly. It is very easy to tame and finger train. No pet can be more satisfying to its owner than this affectionate and lovable companion.

▶ A Pied Cockatiel. Cockatiels are among the most inexpensive parrot-like birds on the market, and are available in most pet shops. They are very adaptable birds that tame easily and are relatively quiet.

◀ Most cockatiels enjoy bathing. Be sure to provide a large enough vessel so that the bird may bathe easily. Some cockatiels will prefer a spray bath to an open dish. Trial and error is the only way to know what your bird likes best.

◀ Perches of various diameters promote exercise that prevents foot problems from occurring. Some types also help to keep the nails of the bird at the proper length.

PURCHASING A COCKATIEL

Before purchasing a cockatiel allow yourself sufficient time to shop around at various pet shops and private breeders to ensure that you have had a good selection. The bird you choose should not sit lethargically, be underweight, or appear wet around the vent area. Birds that are fairly active, have a sleek outward appearance, and show an interest in food are the ones to choose. For the unexperienced bird owner, a very young bird is easier to train. Ask questions as to the bird's age and how long it has been away from its parents. Cockatiels are weaned from the nest anywhere from 6-10 weeks old and should be monitored by the breeder for another 2 weeks to ensure that the bird has been eating on its own. The ideal age to buy your new pet cockatiel is therefore anywhere from 8-12 weeks.

◄ Be certain that all foods given to your cockatiel are safe, especially green foods, from insecticides and pesticides. In addition, do not allow your cockatiel access to your household plants.

▶ The eyes of a healthy pet cockatiel are clear and bright at all times. Any sign of wetness around the eye area, or a bird that sits with its eyes closed, is an indication that the bird is not feeling well.

The popularity of the cockatiel continues to increase as more people come to appreciate its personality and beauty. Because of its docile temperament and its size, the cockatiel has become a favorite among bird owner s. ◄

PURCHASING A COCKATIEL

➥ The Normal Cockatiel is still, despite the introduction of new color varieties, the most popular and inexpensive color variety.

➥ Cockatiels are easiest to tame when they are young. Most young birds have been handled while still in the nest and are therefore used to the human touch.

➥ Take time to observe the individual birds available before choosing a pet cockatiel. Before long, differences in temperament among birds become apparent.

GRAY VARIETIES

The "wild type" or "Normal" Cockatiel, from which all other mutations arose, is predominantly gray in color. Its plumage is hardly competition to the more colorful mutations, but color has nothing to do with the personality of the bird. The Normal Cockatiel is the most common and most inexpensive variety of cockatiel found on the market.

Cockatiels are among the most affectionate and easily tamed of the smaller parrot-like birds. They prefer to cuddle with their owner rather than be rough housed. ◂

◂ The feather colors vary greatly among gray birds from a deep slate gray to a light silver tone. The difference in color variation can be due to variation in diet, territorial region, or climate.

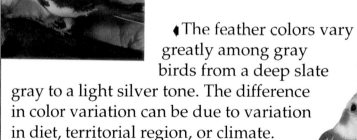

▸ Normal male cockatiels have prominent yellow coloring about their face, and very bright, distinctive red colored cheek patches. They also possess no barring on the underside of their feathers as do the females.

GRAY VARIETIES

The gray coloring varies from dark, charcoal gray, to a lighter, almost silver color. A young Normal Cockatiel will have coloring resembling that of an adult female. Because of this, there is no way to determine the sex of a cockatiel before it goes through its first molt at approximately 4-6 months of age.

Most cockatiels that are taken into households as pets are of the Normal variety. All color mutations are equal in their potential as tame pets.

Apart from hulling seeds, a cockatiel's beak is designed to tear large pieces of food into smaller ones. An untamed cockatiel, or one that feels threatened, can puncture skin when biting to ward off its attacker.

This cockatiel was given the opportunity to roam the house, but chose to stay on top of his cage. A cockatiel will not often leave the vicinity of its cage because it feels secure there.

LUTINO VARIETY

When the Lutino mutation was established it immediately overtook bird fanciers hearts because it very much resembled the large white Cockatoo that was quite a considerable amount of money. This, to many, was a miniature version of the bird that they so longed to have, but could not afford. The Lutino Cockatiel is not white in color, but actually a pale yellow.

➧ Note how the Lutino Cockatiel maintains the yellow and orange coloration on its head. Good color can be maintained with a well balanced diet.

➦ Cockatiels are elegant looking birds with an erect carriage and magnificent crest, which are only two of their many appealing characteristics.

Before placing a pair of cockatiels together for breeding, be sure that the they are genetically compatible for the result you have in mind. ➧

LUTINO VARIETY

All Lutinos have dark, red eyes, a yellow head and crest, bright red cheek patches, and predominantly creamy white feathers on the rest of their body and wings. A characteristic that occurs in the Lutino, and is no cause for the owner to worry, is a small bald spot directly behind the crest on the top of the head. It is a natural, dominant trait that breeders have tried to abolish for years and still have not been successful.

Lutino Cockatiels are beautiful birds, but a dominant genetic factor is a bald spot directly behind its crest. This is common in all Lutino's and is no cause for alarm.

▲ Although some Lutinos seem to lack yellow pigmentation, they are not considered Albino.

A Lutino still has pigmentation in its cheeks as well as the underparts of the wing.

▲ Adult Lutinos are more difficult to sex than Normal colored adults. To sex a Lutino, the wing must be extended or the underside of the tail feathers must be made visible.

Because of the lack of pigment in their eyes, Lutinos often appear to be sensitive to bright light. ◀

PIED VARIETY

The Pied mutation was the first to occur. Some breeders refer to it as variegated. This "marbled" colored bird is similar in color to the Normal, but has light yellow patches of different sizes that interrupt the dark color. The most perfect Pied has complete symmetry to its patches. The markings of a Pied cannot be predicted nor bred for. All Pieds have different markings, no two are alike. Two, very well marked birds that are to be bred together can not guarantee the young that they will produce will be nicely marked. Of all cockatiel mutations, the Pieds are the most difficult to sex. Usually one must rely on distinctive characterizations of a male, or wait to see if the bird lays an egg to verify it is a female.

▶ Birds that have symmetrical markings are most preferred and more expensive. This is because a nicely marked Pied is very difficult to breed for.

No two Pied Cockatiels are alike in their markings and it is impossible to predict the markings of future nestlings from a pair. ▲

The Pied Cockatiel is not a sex-linked mutation. Before a Pied may be produced, both parents must carry the gene factor. A Pair of Normal Cockatiels, split to pied, will both carry the gene, and can produce Pied offspring.

▸

PIED VARIETY

Although the Pied Cockatiel was the first mutation to occur, they are still considered rare. The demand for this uniquely colored cockatiel has increased greatly.

Individual personalities vary greatly between birds, and no one variety of cockatiel makes a better pet than the other. For the most part, all cockatiels are very affectionate and the selection is truly a matter of preference. ▶

Of all cockatiel mutations, the Pieds are the most difficult to sex. Because the markings of each bird vary, there is no consistant pattern to which the determination of sex can be based.

▲ Never leave your pet cockatiel out when no one is home. It is best to safely restrain it in a cage when you are away. This will ensure that the bird will not get into mischief or injured while you are out.

PEARL VARIETY

The Pearl mutation was actually an accident that had occurred in breeding, but it has grown to be quite popular. The best example of a Pearl is a bird that shows a narrow border of gray margining a white or yellow feather giving a scalloped appearance. When the basic yellow background color is a deep yellow, it is referred to as "Gold Laced".

The Pearl Cockatiel is characterized by the way in which each feather is centrally spotted, or outlined, in yellow or white. Because a male Pearl loses his spots after the first molt, banding is essential.

The "pearls" of a bird are most evident on the head, shoulders, wings, and back. The underside, or belly markings are not as prominent as those of the back.

The Pearl mutation was actually an unexpected happening. Breeders are learning how to perfect this mutation, and are creating more and more variations of it.

PEARL VARIETY

A weak yellow is called "Silver Laced". As with the Pied mutation, no two Pearls have the same markings. A very unique feature, of the male Pearl, is that upon molting for the first time the lacings are lost and it resembles a Normal, grey colored, male. This does not mean that it is now considered to be a Normal, it still carries the Pearl gene.

This Pearl Cockatiel has an attractive pale yellow background color. There is great variation in the quality of the markings among Pearl Cockatiels.

The cockatiel does not generally utilize its foot as a hand for holding its food, as do many hookbills. When it occasionally does, it lacks the dexterity that other parrots display.

Youngsters from the same nest are rarely exactly alike and parents that have produced splendidly marked youngsters one year may not repeat this success.

Regardless of color variety, a cockatiel remains basically the same interesting and intelligent pet. Each bird is as individual in its personality as humans are.

NEW VARIETIES

New varieties of cockatiels are constantly being introduced. Some, as this Lutino Pearl, are not very common and are more expensive than the Normal variety.

Several new varieties have been introduced into the bird world such as Cinnamon, White-faced, and variations of the Pearl. Of these, the Cinnamon is the most common. It is actually a pale, brownish-gray color. The White-faced Cockatiel lacks any trace of yellow in the mask and body and has no orange in the cheek patches. Its head and shoulder patches are totally white and its body is typically gray.

All Cinnamon Cockatiels have pinkish, flesh colored eyes when they are first hatched. As they mature, their eyes change to a medium brownish color, as opposed to the deep brown or black of the Normals.

This is a new color variety of the cockatiel combining the Pearl, Cinnamon, and White-faced mutations. Breeders aim to eventually produce consistent heavy pearling, as well as males that will retain their pearl markings in adult plumage.

The Cinnamon Cockatiel is a dilute mutation of the Normal.

Adult male cockatiels acquire more melanin than hens or youngsters, and therefore the darkest shades of cinnamon are seen in the adult male.

NEW VARIETIES

The Pearl Cockatiel, although a mutation itself, also has variations that are beginning to be introduced to the bird world; Pearl White-faced, Pearl Cinnamon, and Pearl Lutino. Breeders are still ever hopeful of a spontaneous happening of an all white bird, the Albino. An Albino will have no pigmentation in it what-so-ever. As we know it, this has not yet occurred.

Cinnamon is a sex-linked mutation. A good Cinnamon is almost light brown in color. The predominant feather coloration is silver to tan. There is considerable variation because the bird's genes affect the intensity of its color. ➥

White Cockatiel. A true Albino Cockatiel will lack all pigmentation. This cockatiel has dark colored eyes. ➤

White-faced Cockatiels lack any trace of yellow in the mask and body. They preserve only melanin. Some find this unattractive because the birds lack the pretty, orange cheek patches. ➥

CAGES

Although not appearing very large, a cockatiel requires a great deal of space in its cage. Wooden cages are not recommended because of the need a cockatiel has to chew. Round cages are also not advisable unless the diameter is greater than 24 inches.

◆ Today, cages are made with food and water cups accessible from the outside. This is a nice attribute because not a lot of commotion is made during the changing of the food and water.

Birds should be supervised at all times while they are out of their cage. Cockatiels are curious creatures that are bound to get into mischief if you are not around to stop them. ◆

◆ Birds that are to be housed singly and not tamed should have toys or hanging treats in their cage to keep them occupied. The number of accessories that will be placed into a cage must be taken into consider-ation before the cage is purchased so that the proper cage size is acquired. ▶

◀ If your pet cockatiel will be out of its cage for a while, you may want to have some food and water available for it. Little tidbits of food that you are enjoying make nice treats for your bird.

CAGES

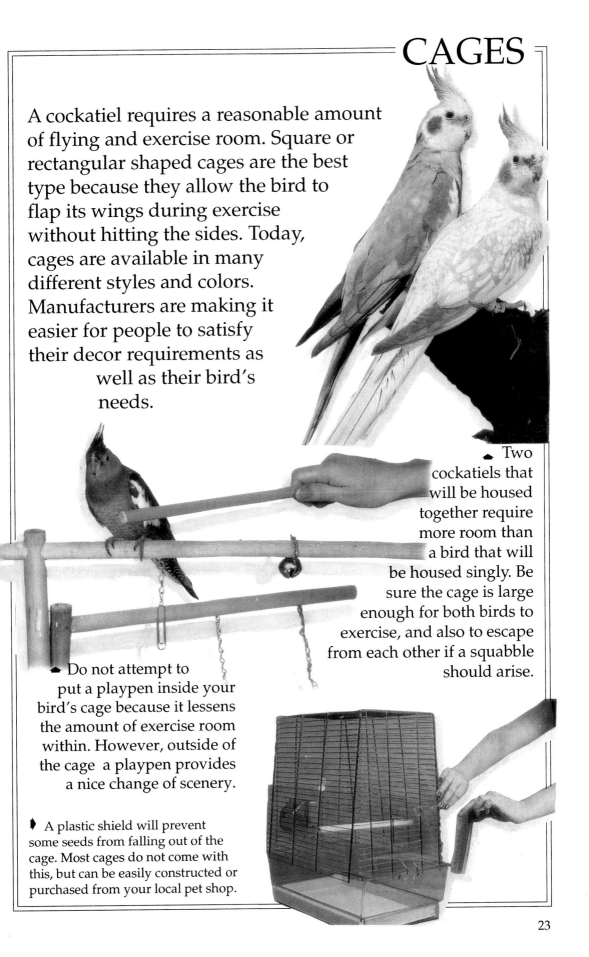

A cockatiel requires a reasonable amount of flying and exercise room. Square or rectangular shaped cages are the best type because they allow the bird to flap its wings during exercise without hitting the sides. Today, cages are available in many different styles and colors. Manufacturers are making it easier for people to satisfy their decor requirements as well as their bird's needs.

◆ Two cockatiels that will be housed together require more room than a bird that will be housed singly. Be sure the cage is large enough for both birds to exercise, and also to escape from each other if a squabble should arise.

◆ Do not attempt to put a playpen inside your bird's cage because it lessens the amount of exercise room within. However, outside of the cage a playpen provides a nice change of scenery.

▶ A plastic shield will prevent some seeds from falling out of the cage. Most cages do not come with this, but can be easily constructed or purchased from your local pet shop.

AVIARIES

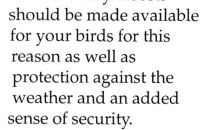

An aviary provides plenty of exercise room for your bird. Usually, a cockatiel will attempt to climb to the highest possible place in the aviary. Roosts should be made available for your birds for this reason as well as protection against the weather and an added sense of security.

Cockatiels breed very well in an aviary. Territorial disputes can occur when two or more pairs are housed together. There should be more nest boxes supplied in an aviary than pairs of birds to keep squabbling to a minimum.

Perches of either natural tree branches or smooth dowels should be provided within the aviary to allow cockatiels to rest. These must be free of insecticides and pesticides and cannot be otherwise toxic to your birds.

Some townships have zoning laws that do not permit aviaries to be built. Check with your town before you begin to build one. It is also advised to inform your neighbors of your intentions so that they will have no complaints about a new structure.

Cockatiels are one of the few birds that prove to do well in both cages and aviaries. There are a few considerations involved in building an aviary for your cockatiel. First, a suitable site. A location which is partially sheltered from strong prevailing winds and direct sunlight is most desirable. Secondly, the floor of the aviary should be made of cement to keep rodents from burrowing up and through. Probably the most important consideration is size. Of course, the bigger the better, but it should be at least the size of a chicken coop. Proper protection should be added to the aviary during the winter months. A heavy plastic may be attached to the frame of the aviary to block the cold and snow.

◀ The nutritional requirements for birds kept in an aviary are the same as for those kept indoors. They should be given daily feedings of seed and water, and additional fruits and vegetables for added vitamins and nutrients.

▶ A well planned aviary can add a decorative touch to your property, and your birds will benefit from it as well.

Every aviary should be equipped with a shelter to provide protection from prolonged sunlight, wind, rain, and extreme temperatures.
◀

GENERAL CARE

On the floor of the cage, place a small handful of loose gravel on top of a sheet of plain paper sized to line the bottom. Gravel is eaten by the bird to aid it in digestion.

◀ Fresh food and water should always be available for your bird. Be sure that good seed is showing for your bird and not just husks. Birds shell their seeds, throw the empty shells on top of perfectly good seed, and then do not dig down underneath the shells to get to good food.

▲ Breeding birds require extra food. Eggs and starchy foods not only put weight on your birds, but are sufficient for parent birds to feed their young.

Preening is a natural act that a cockatiel will do daily. Cockatiels that do not enjoy bathing will preen more often. ◀

A spoiled cockatiel enjoys eating from its owner's hand. If the bird becomes accustomed to this, it can create a habit of it. ◀

A proper diet and a sufficient amount of exercise will keep your bird in top condition. The best way to ensure that your bird receives a good diet is to make it as varied as possible.

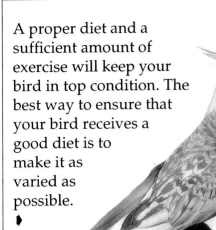

▶ This bird is well fed. Its belly feathers actually show an indentation to its breast bone because of the layer of fat on the breast. A poorly fed or underweight bird shows the breast bone protruding.

Upon bringing home your new pet cockatiel it is important that the diet it has been receiving is duplicated. Cockatiels are not ones to accept new foods too quickly and it may actually go a few days without eating if its diet has been changed. ◄

The cockatiel is a ground eating bird and goes down to the floor of the cage to pick through the pebbles. A good mixture of seeds should be provided for the bird in two open, relatively large seed vessels. Water is best if it is spring or distilled and should be placed in a smaller vessel than the food, and higher in the cage so that it will stay cleaner. A small night light should always be left on for your bird because cockatiels frighten easily and may injure themselves in the cage during the night if they cannot see.

MAINTENANCE

Cockatiels require very little maintenance outside of daily food and water and a clean kept cage. Occasionally a cockatiel requires its beak or nails to be trimmed because of overgrowth. An overgrown beak can become serious if left unattended. When it becomes too long, the bird will not be able to shell its seed to eat. Long nails can also pose problems. They tend to get caught in the wire of the cage or on carpets and drapes which can lead to broken legs. There are times when a cockatiel's nails may appear as needlepoints, but will not actually be long enough to cut. In this case, a nail file may be used to file the tips off.

Clipping a beak of a bird is not very common. If yours appears to be overgrown, take it to an expert for verification. Do not attempt to trim this yourself because the beak is fragile. If not clipped correctly it may shatter. ▶

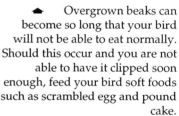

◆ Overgrown beaks can become so long that your bird will not be able to eat normally. Should this occur and you are not able to have it clipped soon enough, feed your bird soft foods such as scrambled egg and pound cake.

Sometimes a bird's nails do not require clipping. A simple filing with a household emery board is sufficient enough to remove the tips of the nails. ▶

➡ Whether it is a simple filing or a clipping of either the beak or the nails, a cockatiel does not care to have this done, and will sometimes hold a grudge against the person who performed the job.

◀ A bird's wing requires clipping after every molt. Sometimes a bird will be able to fly when only one or two feathers has grown back.

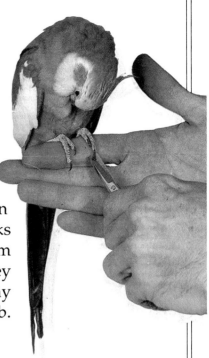

The proper way to hold your cockatiel, during such procedures, is important to know. It will make the experience of clipping the nails, beak, or wings much better for the bird and owner.

Birds sometimes wear down their own beaks and nails from the things they eat and the way they climb.

If you are lucky, your bird will allow you to clip its nails while perched on your hand. Nail clipping can be accomplished with a pair of clippers purchased from your local pet shop.

Not much is lost in the bird's appearance when the wings are clipped. It is a completely painless process which the bird does not even realize has been done. Keep the bird low to the ground the first time it is let out of its cage after its wing is clipped. The bird will try to fly, and may become injured if it does not realize that it cannot.

Before breeding your birds, file their nails so that the eggs are not accidentally broken in the nest. This should be done well in advance to the breeding season.

DIET

A good seed mixture is required to provide your cockatiel with the basic nutrients and vitamins required to maintain top condition. Seed mixtures made up by a private breeder or a pet shop are best. These will consist of a variety of small seeds such as millet, canary, hulled oats, flax, and hemp. Sunflower and safflower seeds can also be added to your bird's diet. In addition to the regular seed, fruits and vegetables provide important vitamin supplements to your bird's well being. Table foods that are starchy and high in protein such as pasta, rice, and breads are very advantageous to the overall condition of your bird.

Cockatiels in the wild go to the ground to eat. Food and water can be placed in vessels located higher in the cage, but birds prefer it on the floor. ◂

Seed bells and other treats are little extra forms of food that can be given to your bird in addition to its regular diet. They should not be the only source of food made available to your bird. ▸

◂ If your bird is left out of its cage most of the day, place some food outside the cage so that it may eat occasionally.

A variety of fruits and vegetables provide your bird with extra vitamins and nutrients. Darker greens, such as spinach and escarole, are higher in their nutrient content than lettuce. Be sure your bird eats plenty of its regular seed. If you should find that it is consuming more "treats," cut down on the amount you are giving it. Cockatiels need to eat a seed mixture because of the protein it contains. ➤

Some people actually set an extra place for their bird at the dinner table! This makes the bird feel as if it is eating just as you are, and it stops it from begging for some of your food. ➤

Too many greens can make your bird's droppings appear loose. If you are aware that your bird has been eating extra greens the resulting diarrhea is no cause for alarm.

Young cockatiels should not be given too many greens and fruits. They require more seed to give them the calories needed for growth and to maintain a healthy weight. ➤

➤ Grains and sprouted seeds are enjoyed and prove to be healthy for your bird. These should be properly cured to ensure against mold.

WING CLIPPING

Too many tragic accidents have occurred from not having the wing of a pet cockatiel clipped. Trimming your bird's wing is good insurance that it will not fly into mirrors or windows or out of an open door. (Not to mention into a hot pot cooking on the stove!) Wing clipping requires upkeep. If the feathers of the wing are not clipped after every molt, the bird will be able to fly again.

▶ A full winged bird is difficult to train. By clipping the wing, more time is actually spent handling the bird during training.

◀ Only one wing of the bird should be clipped. This unbalances it. If both wings are clipped, the bird will still be able to fly.

The wing of your bird should always be clipped, even after the bird is tame. This keeps the bird dependant upon you for certain things, in turn, making a better pet. ▶

WING CLIPPING

To do so, hold the bird securely with only one wing extended for clipping. A regular pair of household scissors may be used. The primary feathers, from approximately the seventh feather from the back up, are cut. Cutting the feathers in this manner allows the bird to break its fall when it attempts to fly, but not gain any altitude.

➤ A full winged bird should never be taken out of the house. Even the tamest of birds has flown away from excitement or freight, and some very good pets have been lost.

If unsure how to clip the wing of your pet cockatiel, take it to a private breeder, pet shop, or veterinarian so that the proper way to hold and clip the bird may be demonstrated. It may cost a little, but it will better future wing clipping experiences. ➤

➤ Wing clipping is painless. The first time a bird is let out of its cage after its wing has been clipped, keep it low to the ground. The bird does not know that it cannot fly and may injure itself by trying to do so.

Cockatiels act as if everything is a traumatic experience. Speak softly to your bird during and after the process as a reassurance that all is okay. ▶

HAND TAMING

A bird that is purchased and brought home to new surroundings requires 7-10 days to settle in and become accustomed. Be sure that the bird is eating well before you begin to handle it. Upon first taking the bird out of the cage, do not grab it with your hands, either let it come out by itself, or throw a towel over it to remove it. Work close to the floor and in a corner, so the bird cannot escape. Cup the bird gently in your hands, applying no pressure. Gently try to scratch the top of the bird's head and neck.

Sometimes training is easier if you use a perch to force the bird to step up. Gradually move your hand in closer on the perch. Eventually the cockatiel will be sitting on your hand.

When a bird is cupped in your hand and no pressure is being applied, it will not bite you. This actually makes the bird feel more secure.

While the bird is sitting on your hand, try to relax it by scratching along its head, neck, and back. Most cockatiels enjoy this. You will want to begin scratching the bird around the chin, and work your way around to the back of its neck. This way the cockatiel will be able to see your hand and will know exactly what you are doing. Reaching directly to the back of the neck frightens the bird.

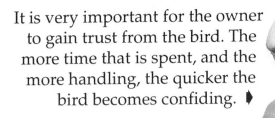

It is very important for the owner to gain trust from the bird. The more time that is spent, and the more handling, the quicker the bird becomes confiding. ▶

Young cockatiels are the easiest to tame. If handled while still in the nest, they become accustomed to people and require little taming. ▶

◀ Upon beginning training keep the bird low to the ground so that it does not fly off of your hand and hurt itself.

◀ Once a cockatiel is tame, the more people that handle it, the better. However, it is best if only one person initially trains the bird.

After scratching the bird on its head, attempt to have the bird sit in the palm of your hand without jumping off. Once the bird stays in your hand attempt to make it step up onto your finger. You are well on your way to a tame pet cockatiel!

TOYS

Toys provide activity for your bird. If you are not home for the most part of the day, it is a good idea to have some sort of play toy in your bird's cage. There are a variety of toys on the market. Choose toys that are specifically designed for small parrots. Be advised against sharp objects or anything that your bird may get caught on.

◀ Before you place a toy in the bird's cage, be sure that there are no sharp edges or areas that your bird can become hooked on. Paperclips, and certain types of snaps can be dangerous to your bird.

Ladders are great fun for cockatiels, but they do not always know how to climb them. A good teaching method is to hold a favorite treat above the bird so that it has to step up to reach. After it does so, give the bird the treat as a reward. ▶

Toys come in a variety of colors and sizes. Like humans, cockatiels have favorite colors too. What your bird's favorite color is can only be learned from studying what color toys it seems to play with most. ▶

◀ It is normal for a bird not to play with a toy when it is first introduced to the cage. Cockatiels are a bit leery of new objects but once accustomed, it quickly becomes a favorite.

▶

Cockatiels sometimes keep themselves entertained for hours playing with the same toy. If a "favorite" toy breaks, or becomes so worn out that it must be thrown away, a bird will "cry," tiny squealing noises, when it is no longer there.

TOYS

There are times when a common toothpick will keep your bird entertained for hours. If your bird is not yet tame, or if you are attempting to teach it to talk, toys are not advisable. They take the bird's attention away from you. Toys are designed to eliminate boredom and to occupy the bird's time when you are not there. A tame bird will prefer to play with its owner rather than the toys it has in its cage.

← Some toys are not designed for cockatiels.
Wood toys must be soft enough so that the cockatiel is able to chew it. A toy that cannot be chewed, is only clutter in the cage.

◀ Common things will amuse your bird for hours. Some of their favorites are leaves, toothpicks, pen caps, and paper.

More brightly colored toys seem to catch the attention of cockatiels before dull colored ones. ➤

◀ Some toys can be quite expensive. You may want to think twice before spending too much money if you think your bird will only destroy something in a matter of minutes.

EXERCISE

As common exercise, a cockatiel will hang against the side of the cage and flap its wings for a few minutes out of the day. If your bird is not given sufficient room do this within its cage, it should be allowed out so that it may stretch properly. A full winged bird should be accustomed with windows and doors so that it will not harm itself by flying into them when it is let out of its cage. There are times that you may allow your bird to come out and it will only want to sit on top of its cage. This is okay, it is still a form of exercise as well as a change of scenery.

◆ Two cockatiels that are housed together, in a small cage, require time out to get the proper amount of exercise. At times, the birds will simply sit on top of their cage, but they are still receiving exercise.

◆ A tame cockatiel receives plenty of exercise if you take it out of its cage to play with it. It may be a good idea to let it roam about, with your supervision, so that it can investigate its environment.

◆ Cockatiels can get into mischief if they are left unsupervised. When permitted out of their cage, be certain that household plants are not available for them to gnaw on, most are poisonous.

◆ It may seem that every time you look at your aviary birds they may be puerched, but flying around an aviary one or two times provides cockatiels with plenty of exercise.

◄ A bird that is permitted to exercise is a healthy bird. A bird that is confined to its cage is more likely to gain weight, which can pose future health problems.

◄ When a cockatiel is let out of its cage, it may not make full use of the room, but prefers only certain places to walk and perch.

◄ Before you allow your bird to fly free throughout the house, be sure that it is familiar with doors and windows so that it does not injure itself by flying into or out of one.

A little ingenuity on the part of the owner can make the time a bird stays out of its cage fun and interesting. Specially designed perches or playpens are wonderful ways to achieve this. ▶

TALKING

Cockatiels are not prolific talkers but can be taught a few words as well as short sentences. Both the male and female have the ability to talk. The key to having any bird talk is constant repetition of the word or phrase you are trying to teach. Naturally, the first word is the most difficult to learn. Only one word should be taught at a time so that the bird does not become confused.

◀ The cockatiel is not a prolific talker but it can be taught to repeat a number of words and short sentences. To teach your bird to talk takes a great deal of patience and time.

▲ Training your cockatiel to talk requires an unusual amount of time. There is no set time limit; some learn faster than others.

Mirrors and toys should be removed from the bird's cage when attempting to teach it to talk. The full attention of the bird is necessary if you intend to have it mimic what you are saying. ▶

▲ Teaching a cockatiel to talk is best carried out in an environment free of distractions. Talking and imitation often take place when the bird is resting and relaxed. This is the time to teach it to talk.

The full attention of your cockatiel is required for it to learn to speak. If you talk while the bird is examining some object or listening to another sound, you are wasting time. Cockatiels are proficient whistlers. They can learn lengthy tunes, but the more they whistle, the less they talk. Whistling is much easier to learn, and they are pleased by your approval so they will continue to whistle and not talk well.

↑ It does not matter what age you begin to teach your bird to talk. Birds have been known to talk as early as 14 weeks old.

↑ The color variety of your cockatiel has no affect on its talking ability. All color varieties have the ability to speak.

↑ Cockatiels are very capable of whistling tunes. It is much easier for a cockatiel to learn a tune than to mimic a phrase. If you wish to teach your bird to speak, do not allow it to learn to whistle.

A COCKATIEL'S FEATHERS

Healthy and fully developed plumage is essential to the well being of your pet. Contour feathers are the most numerous of the various feather types. These form the outer covering that give the cockatiel its shape. Flight feathers are specialized contour feathers that are found on the wings and tail.

→ Contour feathers are the most numerous and the most conspicuous of the various types. These form the outer covering and give the cockatiel its characteristic shape.

◀ Located next to the skin is a fluffy coating of down. This is especially important for insulation. A newly hatched cockatiel has yellow down on its back, and an adult generally has white.

The flight feathers of this drawing are color coded. The primaries and secondaries are brown, the greater coverts blue, and the lesser coverts red. ▶

A COCKATIEL'S FEATHERS

Another important feather type in parrots and other birds is the fluffy coating of down which is located next to the skin underlying the contours. These are especially important for the birds insulation. During cold weather and sickness, birds "fluff" their feathers to trap body heat within the down layer.

Molting is the process by which all feathers are shed and subsequently replaced by new ones. In the cockatiel, it is a very gradual process which extends over a period of several months. ▶

▲ The bones associated with the limbs are colored blue.

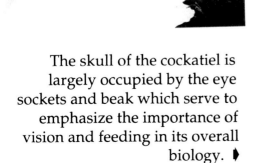

The skull of the cockatiel is largely occupied by the eye sockets and beak which serve to emphasize the importance of vision and feeding in its overall biology. ▶

DETERMINING SEX

The sex of young birds cannot be determined until after their first molt when they receive their adult plumage. In most varieties of cockatiels, the sex can be determined from a wing or tail feather. If the tail feathers are of solid color, the bird is a male.

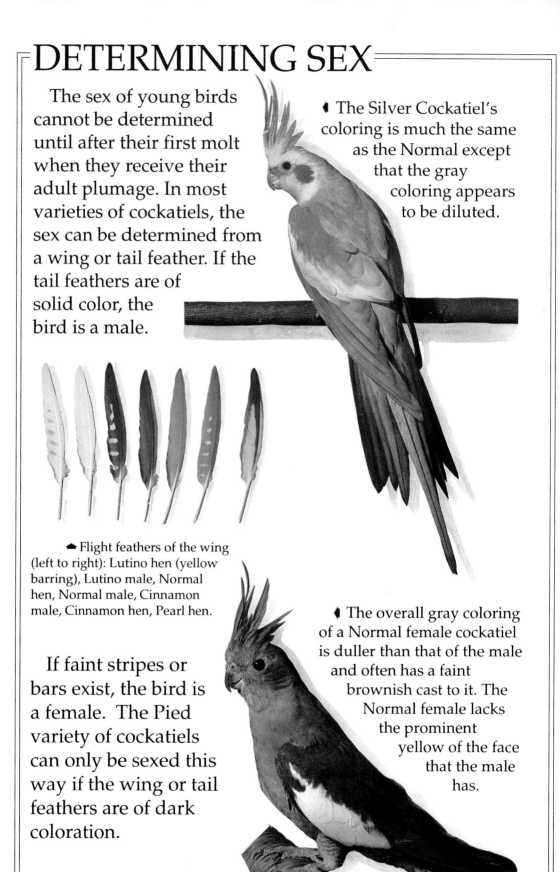

◀ The Silver Cockatiel's coloring is much the same as the Normal except that the gray coloring appears to be diluted.

◆ Flight feathers of the wing (left to right): Lutino hen (yellow barring), Lutino male, Normal hen, Normal male, Cinnamon male, Cinnamon hen, Pearl hen.

If faint stripes or bars exist, the bird is a female. The Pied variety of cockatiels can only be sexed this way if the wing or tail feathers are of dark coloration.

◀ The overall gray coloring of a Normal female cockatiel is duller than that of the male and often has a faint brownish cast to it. The Normal female lacks the prominent yellow of the face that the male has.

DETERMINING SEX

Another way you can determine the sex of an adult bird is to turn the bird upside down and place your finger over the vent; you will feel two bony ridges. In the male they are very close together, females have a wider space between the ridges and have a feel of flexibility.

◀ A female Pearl retains her beautiful coloring all her life. There are several varieties of the Pearl mutation that exist; Pied Pearl, Lutino Pearl, and Fawn Pearl.

The front of the Normal male's head, cheeks, and throat are lemon yellow. The sides of the head are white with large red-orange patches. The general body color of the Normal female is much like the male except that the wing bars and eye patches are less pure in color. ◀

➤ The difference between the male and female Lutino is not recognizable unless the wings of a mature bird are extended. A male Lutino will have no markings on the inside of its wing while a female will have yellow barring.

The Pearl mutation is unique in that the male Pearl loses his spots as he matures. This does not always happen after the first molt. By the second year he appears as a Normal colored male. In breeding he is, of course, a pure Pearl.

BREEDING CONDITION

Male and female cockatiels that are separated prior to breeding have noticeable characteristics that inform us they are ready to breed. A male cockatiel begins to whistle quite often and heartily while holding its wings out from the body. Aggressive males will begin squabbling among one another. Female cockatiels crouch down on the perch in a typical mating stance.

➡ The best breeding results are achieved from breeding birds no younger than 18 to 24 months old. Mature birds can be expected to produce healthy young for 4 or 5 seasons.

Cockatiels come into breeding condition if they are given a well balanced diet and allowed to exercise adequately.

Although some mutations are the result of inbreeding, closely related stock should not be bred together. Only very experienced breeders who have special knowledge of inbreeding and have a definite objective in view should inbreed their birds. ▶

46

BREEDING CONDITION

Both sexes become more active and are alert to calls from the opposite sex. A pair of cockatiels that has been kept together does not show such obvious signs. However, if a nest box is in place, they will become interested in it and the male will begin to court the female.

→ One purpose of courtship is to stimulate the reproductive process of the hen. A male cockatiel does not display elaborate courtship behavior. He will however, whistle a tune to the hen and act out a dance.

→ Cockatiels are universally considered one of the most free-breeding members of the parrot family.

◆ Cockatiels have particularly strong pair bonds. It is generally accepted that in the wild a pair may remain together until death separates them.

PAIRING

Cockatiels are old enough to begin breeding between one to three years of age. Birds younger than this do not have the proper breeding experience and should be paired with an older, experienced cockatiel that has bred before. The experienced bird will pick up the slack when the youngster falls behind in his or her duties.

➤ An advanced breeder may want to conduct experimental pairing with his stock. By doing so, he may be able to produce a new variety or mutation of the cockatiel. Very detailed records must be kept in such processes.

➤ Pairs that are to be mated together for the first time should be given 5 to 7 days to become properly acquainted before giving them a nest box.

➤ Wild cockatiels are frequently reported as nesting in extremely small cavities. Considering the average size clutch of cockatiel babies, 4-10, and the size they attain while still within the nest, an artificial nest box that they use is also considered small.

Cockatiels are relatively easy to breed. They usually accept a mate without problems. Occasionally, a bird that has been separated from its former mate, but is still able to see or hear it, will not accept another one in its place. If a pair of birds does not mate after they have had an available nest box for some time, it may be because the pair does not like the location of the box, and it should be moved.

Prior to the actual breeding season, prospective pairings should be made on paper with each bird's pedigree checked against the stock register. ▶

▶ When two or more cockatiels are housed together, they will rarely breed.

➡ Cockatiels will attempt to breed all year 'round. Indoor breeding may take place at anytime during the year. Outdoor aviary birds should be denied the opportunity to breed during the cold parts of the year.

◀ It is often better to pair a cockatiel that is an experienced breeder with one that has not bred before. If the young bird becomes slack in his or her responsibilities, the older one will often take over and set the example.

ADULT NESTING BEHAVIOR

Individual copulatory periods usually last one or two minutes and several may occur in a single day. ◗

➥ Cockatiel pairs spend a lot of time kissing, cooing, grooming, and feeding each other. They will also demonstrate what appears to be genuine affection for their mates.

➥ A pair of cockatiels will want to be together at all times. If separated, they will call loudly to one another in attempt to get back together.

Male Cockatiels usually explore the nest box before the female. After a few days, he will encourage the female to move in. Soon after this eggs usually follow. The male continues to go in and out of the nest box courting and feeding his female.

◖ The male cockatiel will most likely be the first to explore the nesting box. He will investigate, explore, move in, and then encourage the female to come and look around.

ADULT NESTING BEHAVIOR

Mating will take place several times a day, for several days, until a full clutch of eggs are laid. During this time, it is important to keep the cage extremely clean. The female has larger, softer, more odoriferous droppings during the breeding period.

◀ Elaborate mating rituals, which are common in many other birds, are not seen in cockatiels. The male, however, may display a little as he approaches the female.

◀ Parent cockatiels may stop feeding and begin to pluck their young when they want to nest again. If the parents begin to pick on the young too much, the young may need to be separated. This may also require the breeder to hand feed the chicks until they are eating on their own.

◆ The male cockatiel will act more aggressive towards other birds in an aviary during breeding season. When he is not assisting his mate with the young, he will stand guard outside the nest box to ward off all danger.

NEST BOXES

Breeding cockatiels requires a nest box. Cockatiels will lay anywhere from 4-10 eggs and consequently should have a large enough nest box to house both parents and all chicks. Nest boxes are made of wood and have a 3½ in. diameter hole centrally located with a perch underneath for the birds to enter easily.

➤ Nest boxes for cockatiels typically follow this design.

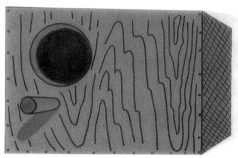

◀ Cockatiels usually spend some time getting acquainted with their new accommodations before actually breeding. They are very suspicious birds that like to investigate everything before trying it.

The placement of the nest is important. It should be easily accessible and convenient for the pair to come and go. It should also be located somewhere where the birds will feel secure. Usually high up in a back corner of the cage is best.

NEST BOXES

An ideal size cockatiel nest box is at least 16x16 in. Pine shavings prove to be sufficient nesting material, and should be packed about 1½ inches deep on the floor. At first placing of the nesting material, ¼ cup of water should be poured over the shavings to provide added moisture. Pack this down and squeeze the excess water out. Once your pair moves in, they will spend much time in the nest. Before long the female will have her eggs laid.

▶ Except when breeding is restricted to warmer months of the year, it is advised that nest boxes be made with tight joints and thick walls and bottom so that they can retain the maximum of heat.

Nest boxes may be mounted in a number of ways. It is best to locate it high up in a corner, and either mounted inside or outside the cage. ▶

◄ A nest box should be of a size large enough to house a pair of birds and anywhere from 4-10 chicks.

In the wild, cockatiels nest in tree cavities. These tree cavities are usually hollowed out by some other type of bird that will not use the same nest cavity twice. ▶

EGG LAYING

Cockatiels lay their eggs approximately every other day. A clutch can contain anywhere from 4-10 eggs, usually averaging 6. The female cockatiel will labor for hours during the laying of one egg, sometimes as much as 10 hours. While she is doing so, the male will sit on the eggs that have already been laid. He will continue to stay with her until she is rested and capable of setting the entire clutch herself. The incubation period for cockatiel eggs is approximately 18 to 19 days.

◄ If a pair, or only one of the birds, does not accept a nest box in a particular location after two weeks, it may be because they do not like the location or the nest box itself.

◄ The average cockatiel nest contains 4-10 eggs.

After about 18 or 19 days, you will begin to hear the chick chirping at the shell as it begins to emerge from the egg. In just a few hours the chick will be completely out. The parents clean the baby and shortly thereafter begin to feed it.

Cockatiel chicks appear to grow while you watch them. Within a few days they will double and triple in size. ▶

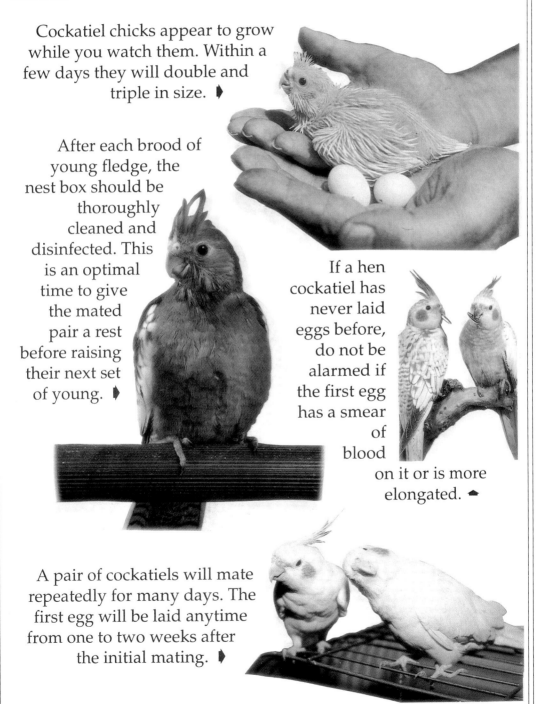

After each brood of young fledge, the nest box should be thoroughly cleaned and disinfected. This is an optimal time to give the mated pair a rest before raising their next set of young. ▶

If a hen cockatiel has never laid eggs before, do not be alarmed if the first egg has a smear of blood on it or is more elongated. ◆

A pair of cockatiels will mate repeatedly for many days. The first egg will be laid anytime from one to two weeks after the initial mating. ▶

DEVELOPMENT OF CHICKS

A newly hatched chick is frail and helpless. It can not raise its head nor open its eyes. Its beak is soft and its body is covered in yellow down. At this stage, the only thing a chick does is cry. It cries when it is disturbed, frightened, hungry, and being fed. At one week old, the feet of a chick begin to color and its eyes begin to open. Approximately 8 days after hatching the chick begins to get pin feathers which give it the ability to retain some heat. At about three weeks old, a chick will begin to climb to the entrance of the nest box to view the outside. At anywhere from 4 to 5 weeks of age it will be able to fly in and out of the nest. The chick will still be receiving food from its parents, but will also practice eating on its own. When a cockatiel chick is eating well enough by itself it can be taken away from its parents.

▲ Young chicks always shuffle themselves backward out from their brothers and sisters and deposit their feces in a ring an inch or two away from the nest hollow.

When the food sacs, known as crops, of the chicks are full and plump, you can be assured they are being well fed. This full appearance should be almost constant.

◀ Young birds need to exercise. To avoid overcrowding, remove individual youngsters away from their parents when they become ready. This is an excellent time for finger taming and training.

DEVELOPMENT OF CHICKS

◀ The baby cockatiel does not gape wide for food. The person hand feeding a cockatiel chick has to work the food in through a narrow opening which makes rearing the young take a little longer than if done by the parents.

➤ The chicks generally do not return to the nest once they have left. Instead, they prefer to perch on the floor of the cage or in a corner, usually in the company of their siblings or parents.

➤ A cockatiel chick requires constant brooding at this age because it cannot maintain its body temperature.

➤ At 4½ weeks old a cockatiel chick is completely covered with feathers.

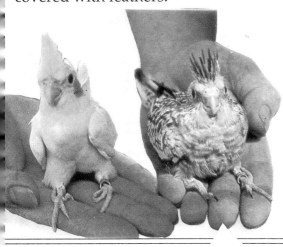

Young birds can safely be removed from their parents at an age of 8 to 10 weeks by which time they should be fully weaned. This chick has at least 7 more weeks to go. ◀

BATHING

In the wild, cockatiels usually bathe in rain showers. This can be imitated in the home by giving the bird a spray bath. Cockatiels do not have to bathe, they are capable of keeping clean through their preening routine. They spend a good part of the day caring for their feathers. The feathers are pulled through the beak and any soiling is cleaned off.

◀ As a cockatiel takes its bath it will usually stretch itself and squeal with delight as it thoroughly wets every part of its body.

◀ Pet cockatiels often want to try the foods their owners enjoy.

Cockatiels are capable of keeping perfectly clean without bathing in water. Cockatiels generally preen and groom several times during the day to keep every feather looking healthy and in place. ▶

The natural powder down that is emitted from their bodies is used to clean each and every feather. If you find your cockatiel attempting to bathe in a small water dish, you may place a shallow, heavy bowl in the bird's cage. During breeding, a hen cockatiel will take more frequent baths to keep the humidity level in the nest box high.

← Except when nesting, cockatiels seldom bathe in standing water but they particularly love to be showered by falling spray or rain.

← It is not advisable to bathe young birds. You may find them to be dirty from being inside the nest box but they are more susceptible to illness from drafts at such an early age.

← Cockatiels originated from the dry regions of Australia and therefore did not have much access to water for bathing. A natural powder down helps to keep their feathers clean during preening.

The mother cockatiel bathes frequently while nesting to keep the humidity level in the nest high. ►

MOLTING

Molting is a natural process that occurs approximately twice a year. It is the process by which the feathers of a bird fall out and are replaced. Not all of the feathers fall out at one time. It is a gradual process that usually takes about 2-3 months to complete.

↑
Old, damaged feathers will be replaced with new, healthy ones during molting. To facilitate this process, a bad feather may be pulled out completely in which a new one will grow in within 6 weeks.

← Cockatiels will go through their first molt at 6-8 months of age. At this time the new feather growth will be of the adult coloring.

Cockatiels molt slowly, but once they have their coat, barring accidents and illness, they do not shed. ▶

Molting puts a tremendous amount of stress on the bird; its resistance is lower during this time and it is more susceptible to colds and other illness. Your bird may not chirp as much or appear as active. The best way to facilitate a molt is to keep your pet cockatiel as cool as possible, but not in a draft, and offer a diet that is high in fat; eggs that have been scrambled in butter, toast with butter, noodles with butter, peanut butter, pound cake, etc.

Cockatiels are more susceptible to colds and drafts during their molt. A runny eye or nose is a sign of illness and should be treated as soon as recognized. ◄

A cockatiel will normally molt in the early summer, but this can vary from bird to bird depending on its metabolism and the conditions at which it is kept. ▶

◄ During this process of feather changing, the owner should be aware that the bird's resistance is lowered. Special care should be taken to see that the bird is fed and housed properly.

A cockatiel that is molting will not be as active as usual. Because of all the new feather growth that is taking place, the bird will be listless and calmer than normal. ▶

DISEASE & ILLNESS

A sick bird shows specific signs that informs us it is not feeling well. Sitting with its wings fluffed out to hold in its body temperature, loose droppings, and an overall decline in activity are all signs of the onset of illness. Should this occur, it would be best to move the bird to a "hospital" cage to keep the illness under control.

◀ Fluffed feathers may indicate the onset of illness.

Broken wings must be set, preferably by a veterinarian, to heal properly. At times, a wing may remain slightly drooped if not set correctly or if sprained. During the healing time of this injury, the bird should not be permitted to exercise much. ▶

◀ When the female cockatiel is unable to naturally expel an egg, it is called egg-bound. Heat will relax affected muscles. A heating pad, hospital cage, or holding the bird over steam may help to pass the egg.

DISEASE & ILLNESS

◀ When a contagious disease is affecting a bird that shares a home with one or more birds, separate the ill bird from the cage to prevent spreading.

A "hospital" cage is actually smaller than the bird's everyday cage. It keeps the bird restricted from too much movement. It should be heated to 85-90° F during the treatment of the illness. Food and water should be placed on the floor of the cage because a sick bird will not climb up to eat. Medications for common ailments can be found at your local pet store. More serious cases should be brought to your veterinarian's attention.

Eye infections require obtaining a prescription ointment from your veterinarian. This usually begins with watering of the eyes followed by the surrounding feathers the eyes appearing wet and missing from around the eye area. ▶

Feather picking can be the result of an inadequate diet, lack of room, or boredom. Most times this turns into a habit that can not be broken.

◄ Conjunctivitis causes the eyelids to become swollen to the extent that temporary blindness occurs. Consult your veterinarian at the first signs of watery discharge.

INDEX

Page numbers in **boldface** refer to illustrations.